北齐娄睿墓壁画

山西國寶精華

LOU RUI TOMB MURALS OF THE NORTHERN QI PERIOD

三晋出版社 山西博物院 编

山西出版传媒集团
三晋出版社

问弗
NO.8

《山西国宝精华·北齐娄睿墓壁画》编委会名单

编　　者：三晋出版社　山西博物院
出版统筹：莫晓东
摄　　影：厉晋春
撰　　文：姚　香
翻　　译：叶　南
艺术顾问：佟　雨
封面设计：XXL Studio
排版设计：我在文化工作室
出　　品：问弗文化工作室

图书在版编目（CIP）数据

北齐娄睿墓壁画 / 三晋出版社，山西博物院编．
——太原：三晋出版社，2023.6
（山西国宝精华）
ISBN 978-7-5457-2431-8

Ⅰ．①北…Ⅱ．①三…②山…Ⅲ．①墓室壁画—太原
—北齐—图集 Ⅳ．① K879.412

中国版本图书馆 CIP 数据核字（2022）第 254347 号

山西国宝精华·北齐娄睿墓壁画

编　　者：三晋出版社　山西博物院
责任编辑：张　婷　刘玫吟
助理编辑：王　宇　周瑞程
责任印制：李佳音

出版者：山西出版传媒集团　三晋出版社
地　　址：太原市建设南路 21 号
电　　话：0351-4956036（总编室）
　　　　　0351-4922203（印制部）
网　　址：http://www.sjcbs.cn

经销者：新华书店
承印者：北京雅昌艺术印刷有限公司

开　　本：787mm×1092mm　1/8
印　　张：6.5
字　　数：70 千字
版　　次：2023 年 6 月　第 1 版
印　　次：2023 年 6 月　第 1 次印刷
书　　号：978-7-5457-2431-8
定　　价：198.00 元

如有印装质量问题，请与本社发行部联系　电话：0351-4922268

上架建议：艺术鉴赏
ISBN 978-7-5457-2431-8
定价：198.00 元

历时近 400 年的魏晋南北朝时期是中国历史上政权更迭最频繁的时期，社会动荡，战争不断。这是一个碰撞与融合的时代，又是一个艺术觉醒的时代。在血与火的洗礼中，胡汉之间、南北之间，交流广泛，兼容并包，为隋唐盛世的到来奠定了基础。

北朝时期的山西先后是北魏、东魏、北齐的核心统治区域，也是古代北方民族融合的熔炉、文化汇聚的舞台。北朝后期，尔朱荣和高欢相继以晋阳（今太原）为根基，号令天下。东魏、北齐时期，号为“霸府”“别都”的晋阳权贵云集，政令频出。也因此，晋阳形成了一个生活奢华的贵族阶层和傍附权贵的文化圈层，奢侈之风盛行。

1979 年，北齐东安王娄睿墓在太原被发现，立即轰动了文物考古界和美术史界。据《北齐书》记载，娄睿是一位很有影响力的历史人物。虽贵为皇亲，却因自己过于贪婪，引起朝野怨愤，因而被削官免职，但很快又加官晋爵，步步高升，在晋阳拥有显赫地位和强大权势。娄睿墓规模之大，壁画之精彩，随葬品之丰富，极为罕见，具有重大的历史、艺术、科学价值。尤其是墓中保留下来的北朝壁画，堪称中国南北朝美术考古的重大发现，轰动了中国美术界，填补了中国艺术史上的空白。吴作人先生赞曰：“（娄氏墓的发掘）使千百年来徒凭籍志臆见梗概的北齐绘画，陡见天日；使中国绘画史，犹长河万里，源流更汇支流，空缺得以证实。……观其人物车马，显贵皂隶，非惟各写其形，更顾盼承奉，洋溢其神。……至于壁画之二拙，揆其简练肯定，运笔收纵，承两晋而启隋唐。”

娄睿墓壁画现存 200 余平方米。墓室部分的壁画题材主要是夫妇宴饮、天空星象和神怪异兽等；墓道东、西两壁，天井和甬道的壁画，以绚丽多彩的大型长卷，描绘了墓主人生前的显赫排场，有鞍马游骑、军乐仪仗和门官仪卫等，画面恢宏，人物栩栩如生。鞍马人物，布局紧凑，既分组清楚，又相互呼应；造型准确，既姿态各异，又情趣一致。整幅壁画劲豪雄健，生气盎然，可谓妙得精神、笔迹磊落恣意于墙壁的巨制。

壁画最为精彩的部分当属墓道东、西两壁上的出行图和回归图，画面构图巧妙，错落有致的鞍马人物和载物驼队，前后呼应，一气呵成，俨然一幅气势壮阔的巨幅画卷。东晋顾恺之《论画》曰：“凡画，人最难，次山水、次狗马，台榭一定器尔，难成而易好，不待迁想妙得也。”而娄睿墓壁画不仅人、山水、狗马皆备，且均为妙笔！

娄睿墓壁画采用线描结合色彩晕染的传统手法，用笔纯熟，线条劲挺，不但对轮廓的勾勒准确而简练，而且通过色彩晕染，将对象的体积感与远近景深关系显示了出来。壁画设色均用矿物质颜料，有土红、朱砂、赭石、熟褐、石黄、石青、石绿、墨黑和蛤粉等。色彩纯净稳重，物象渲染与白灰壁面衬映，给传统画法增添了新的表现手法，形成明快、空灵的清新效果。这种手法，导唐墓壁画之先河。谢稚柳先生赞曰：“北齐简而唐略繁。衣纹的表达，唐已不用屈折的描绘而归结于直线及圆转的行笔，且不用尖锋。至于马，如马头，则唐描绘深刻，形神周到。总的艺术情调是：北齐灵动而唐凝重，北齐清高潇洒而唐敦穆，而北齐的风貌是动人的。”

总之，娄睿墓壁画是南北朝时期中国绘画艺术的代表作，填补了中国古代美术史上北朝绘画的空白，其艺术成就上承汉晋，下启隋唐，以草原风格为主，并汲取南朝优长，融合西域画风，兼容并蓄，足以印证北朝艺术的瑰丽气象，在中国绘画史、美术史上留下了光辉的篇章。

The tumultuous period from the Three Kingdoms, the Jin Dynasties and the Sixteen Kingdoms to the Northern and Southern Dynasties, lasting nearly four centuries, witnessed the most frequent regime changes and violent social turmoil in Chinese history. This is an era of clashes and exchanges, but notwithstanding an era of artistic awakening. Along with a baptism of blood and fire came the extensive as well as inclusive cultural and economic exchanges between the north and the south, the "barbarians" and the Han Chinese, which laid the foundation for the arrival of the prosperous Sui and Tang Dynasties.

The Shanxi region during the Northern Dynasties was at the heart of an area controlled by a series of Dynasties including Northern Wei, Eastern Wei and Northern Qi. Since ancient times this was also the place where the nomadic people from the northern steppes came in touch with the Central Plains civilization, which made it a great melting pot of ethnic cultures. During the late period of the Northern Dynasties, northern warlords like Erzhu Rong and Gao Huan made Jinyang (today's Taiyuan) their military base, set out to conquer the world beyond. During Eastern Wei and Northern Qi Dynasties, numerous nobilities and military powers had chosen to station in the city of Jinyang, gradually cultivating a luxurious lifestyle among themselves and a cultural atmosphere admiring splendidness and sophistication, and therefore not surprisingly Jinyang was earned the city nicknames such as "alternative capital" or "hegemonic prefecture".

In 1979, the tomb of Lou Rui was discovered in Taiyuan, immediately causing a sensation in the circles of archaeologists and art historians. According to the Book of the *Northern Qi*, Lou Rui was very much an influential historical figure. As nobility, he was given the royal title Prince Dong'an. Because of his arrogance and greed, he used to attract criticism and hatred from ministers and officials. Nevertheless, his imperial connections ensured his eventual rise to high position. The tomb of Lou Rui is an extremely rare find, considering its grandeur in scale, the brilliance of its mural art, and the rich collection of its funerary wares, all of which are of great historical, artistic and scientific significance. The mural art in particular, a major discovery in the archaeology of art of the Northern and Southern Dynasties, caused a seismic shock in the art circles as well as filled some gaps in the history of Chinese art. The renowned Chinese artist Wu Zuoren once praised the tomb mural as "suddenly bringing to light the long lost paintings of the Northern Qi period, which theretofore could only be grasped through historical records or imagination and guesswork; so that the long history of Chinese painting, just like the long river of thousands of miles, with tributaries coalescing into the mainstream, can now have its missing link reconnected... Look at those different characters, no matter dignitaries or attendants, on horses or in wagons, reaching out or taking in, each not only was depicted of their likeness, but also imbued with human dispositions... As for the quality of the craftsmanship, the mural excelled in its concise and assertive brushwork, which it inherited from the preceding Jin Dynasties and prepared the following Sui and Tang Dynasties thereof."

The tomb of Lou Rui preserved over 200 square meters of murals in total. The murals in the burial chambers are mostly images of celestial atlas, auspicious heavenly animals and banquet scenes dominated by the tomb occupant. The murals on the sidewalls of the entry ramp, in the courtyard and the connecting corridor depict the glorious pageantry of the tomb occupant during his lifetime, with horseback tours, parades of military and ceremonial guards, etc, in a traditional scroll type composition. The representation is magnificent and the characters are lifelike. Horse-riding characters were composed in groups to form a coherent layout, and yet responding to one another; the modeling was accurate, with highly varied postures, yet the overall style was consistent. The artist truly captured the spirits of the characters which are powerful, vigorous and full of vitality, and his brilliant brushworks brought this great work into reality.

The most spectacular job was done on the sidewalls of the tomb ramp, depicting the departure and return of a delegation of riders on horseback. The composition is cleverly laid out with groups of riders, horses and camel caravans overlapping with and responding to each other in a giant scroll unfolding on to the walls. The maestro painter Gu Kaizhi of Eastern Jin Dynasty explained in his work *On Painting*: "Human figures are the most difficult to paint, next are mountains and rivers, and then dogs and horses. Buildings are the easier ones, because they are man-made objects." The murals in the tomb of Lou Rui not only depicted human figures, mountains and rivers, horses, but also did a fantastic job.

The murals adopted the traditional technique of line drawing combined with color shading. The skillful and vigorous brushwork outlines the silhouette succinctly yet accurately, while the color shading suggests volume and brings about a sense of depth. Mineral pigments used for color shadings included ferric oxide, cinnabar, realgar, azurite, malachite, charcoal and powdered shells of clam, and the colors are pure and stable, adding a new expression to the traditional painting, and forming a bright and refreshing effect. This technique opened a new approach to mural paintings that was later inherited by the tomb murals of the Tang Dynasty. The renowned Chinese art connoisseur Xie Zhiliu commented on the Lou Rui tomb murals: "The Northern Qi style is simple while the Tang style is a bit complicated. In Tang Dynasty, straight lines and round strokes are used to represent clothing lines. As for horses, especially their heads, Tang artists depicted them more thoughtfully. The general artistic comparison can be made in that the Northern Qi is lively and clever while Tang is dignified and reserved; Northern Qi elegant while Tang solemn; and the Northern Qi style is so touching."

Generally speaking, the murals of Lou Rui tomb is a representative work of Chinese art in the period of Northern and Southern Dynasties. Their artistic achievement has inherited from the earlier periods of Han and Jin Dynasties, and prepared for the following prosperity of Sui and Tang. The murals make up an important chapter of ancient Chinese art history on the Northern Dynasties that has been long missing. They combined the northern nomadic style with the influences from the Western Regions, and learned from the elegant Southern Dynasties, absorbing and assimilating everything they could to conjure up a glorious piece of work that belongs to the Northern Dynasties art scene.

出行图之鞍马导引图一　墓道西壁中层

Horseback Parade I of the Departure Scene

Middle Section, West Wall of the Entry Ramp

此幅绘导骑二人。前方长者脸修长，戴黑色长裙帽，身穿月白色内衬，外罩月白色右衽窄袖长袍，着细口裤、黑色长靴，腰间束蹀躞带，手扶弓，弓入囊。他坐在枣红色鞍马上，安详凝视前方，纵辔缓行。鞍马络头齐全，鞍鞯俱备。后方从者长圆脸，浓眉凤眼，小胡子，小嘴，头戴黑色长裙帽，身穿枣红色窄袖长袍，着灰白色细口裤、黑色靴。腰间束蹀躞带，佩戴弓。他坐在灰绿色鞍马上，勒住缰绳，正回首观察后续队伍的情况。灰绿色马马首高昂，前腿却步，后腿蹬地，马尾昂扬，作受惊状，竟拉出一串粪便。可见画师十分熟悉草原牧场马的生活习性。

出行图之鞍马导引图一（局部）　墓道西壁中层

Details of Horseback Parade I of the Departure Scene

Middle Section, West Wall of the Entry Ramp

出行图之鞍马导引图一（局部） 墓道西壁中层

Details of Horseback Parade I of the Departure Scene

Middle Section, West Wall of the Entry Ramp

出行图之鞍马游骑图一　墓道西壁中层

Horseback Tour I of the Departure Scene

Middle Section, West Wall of the Entry Ramp

此幅绘鞍马人物一组。左起第一位从骑广额丰颐，椭圆形脸，眉清目秀，高鼻梁，小嘴，头戴黑色长裙帽，身穿右衽窄袖白袍，着细口裤、棕靴。他左手紧勒缰绳，回首窥视。所骑赭色马的长鬃在额头双分，双目有神，络头齐全，鞍鞯俱备。左起第三位为主骑者，脸面修长，浓眉俊眼，高鼻梁，小嘴，连鬓络腮胡，身穿圆领灰白色内衣，外罩赭红色右衽长袍，着细脚裤、高鞡靴，腰束蹀躞带，手执弓，弓入套。从者有三人静静注视着主骑者。最右二人回首后顾，眼神惊骇。

画师通过单层墨线勾画，平涂浓淡色彩和明暗映衬手法，表现出马的健壮体格。马的眼神更是处理得恰到好处。比如离观者最近的这匹枣红马双目炯炯有神，即使观者变换位置，也能感觉到它一直在注视着自己。

出行图之鞍马游骑图一（局部） 墓道西壁中层

Details of Horseback Tour I of the Departure Scene

Middle Section, West Wall of the Entry Ramp

出行图之鞍马游骑图一（局部） 墓道西壁中层

Details of Horseback Tour I of the Departure Scene

Middle Section, West Wall of the Entry Ramp

出行图之鞍马游骑图一（局部） 墓道西壁中层

Details of Horseback Tour I of the Departure Scene

Middle Section, West Wall of the Entry Ramp

出行图之鞍马导引图二　墓道西壁中层

Horseback Parade II of the Departure Scene

Middle Section, West Wall of the Entry Ramp

此幅绘导骑二人。前者策马扬鞭，全神贯注于前方。他广额丰颐，椭圆脸型，浓眉凤眼，高鼻梁，小嘴，头戴黑色长裙帽，穿浅赭色圆领窄袖长袍，着赭色细口裤、黑靴，腰间束蹀躞带，佩弓和弓套。其右手执鞭，左手勒缰绳。所骑的赭红色骏马络头齐全，鞍鞯俱备，下挂虎皮纹障泥。后者年龄稍长，双目盯着前下方，似乎惊慌失措。他广额长脸，浓眉凤眼，大耳，连鬓络腮胡，身穿枣红长袍，腰束蹀躞带，佩褐色鞶囊、弓和长剑。其右手曳缰绳，左手扶剑。所骑枣红马似乎猛然受惊而后缩，马头高扬，前蹄飞跃，后腿下蹲。骑者躬身伏在马背，紧勒缰绳，脚踩马镫，极力控制使之稳定。

鞍马出行图（局部） 墓道西壁中层

Details of the Horseback Departure Scene

Middle Section, West Wall of the Entry Ramp

此幅为墓道西壁中层鞍马出行图局部。后排最左一人面朝前方，眉清目秀，高鼻梁，戴黑色长裙帽。其身侧有二人望向行进的方向。前排的中年人端坐在枣红马上，以手勒马。他丰额广颐，椭圆形脸，眉清目秀，高鼻梁，戴黑色长裙帽，身穿月白色圆领内衣，外罩赭色窄袖右衽长袍。枣红马马首高昂，双耳竖起，长鬃披在左侧，络头齐全。后边另一匹枣红马双眼低视，额头挂红缨，鬃毛整齐。

回归图之鞍马导引图一　墓道东壁中层

Horseback Parade I of the Return Scene

Middle Section, East Wall of the Entry Ramp

此幅绘有二人二马，似为马队前导引者。为首一人转身面对马匹，回望队伍后方，似在观察后方状况，控制队伍行进的节奏。他广额丰颐，椭圆形脸，浓眉大眼，高鼻梁，颌下蓄须，头戴黑色长裙帽，身穿灰白色圆领内衬，外罩灰白色圆领左衽窄袖长袍，腰间束蹀躞带，佩挂弓、弓囊和矢箙。其左手所牵枣红色马络头齐全，鞍鞯俱备。马首左侧有黄色缨，胸前有攀胸，臀部有鞧，白色马鞍下挂灰白色障泥。身旁一人年龄稍长，正全神贯注目视前方，衣着穿戴与前者近似，颌下蓄须，连鬓络腮胡。他手执长弓，牵赭黄色马。马匹齐鬃，黑白相间，马耳高竖向枣红色马转动，额顶有黑色大缨，络头齐全，鞍鞯俱备，红色马鞍下挂灰白色障泥，马前有攀胸，臀部有鞧。二人二马虽交错重叠，但画面将人马关系交代得非常清楚。

回归图之鞍马导引图一（局部） 墓道东壁中层

Details of Horseback Parade I of the Return Scene

Middle Section, East Wall of the Entry Ramp

回归图之鞍马游骑图一　墓道东壁中层

Horseback Tour I of the Return Scene

Middle Section, East Wall of the Entry Ramp

此幅为主骑图，绘有五人五鞍马，密密匝匝，繁而不乱。五人均为中年男性，椭圆脸，浓眉凤眼，高颧骨，高鼻梁，多为八字胡，且留有浓密的络腮胡。他们头戴圆形长裙帽，身穿圆领窄袖长袍，着细口裤、黑色高靿靴。人物或侧脸，或正面，或扭头，可见部分人物腰间束蹀躞带，手扶弓的中部，弓下部插于弓囊。马匹或全身皆露，或仅见马臀，或局部隐约可见，均可相互参照，避免重复。整幅画面将人的威武与马的健硕表现得相得益彰。

回归图之鞍马游骑图一（局部） 墓道东壁中层

Details of Horseback Tour I of the Return Scene

Middle Section, East Wall of the Entry Ramp

回归图之鞍马游骑图一（局部） 墓道东壁中层

Details of Horseback Tour I of the Return Scene

Middle Section, East Wall of the Entry Ramp

回归图之鞍马导引图二　墓道东壁中层

Horseback Parade II of the Return Scene

Middle Section, East Wall of the Entry Ramp

此幅绘有二人二鞍马，为后面马队的导骑。前者为中年男性，广额丰颐，椭圆形脸，浓眉凤眼，高鼻梁，小嘴。他头戴黑色圆形长裙帽，身穿月白色圆领内衬，外罩灰白色圆领右衽长袖长袍，腰束蹀躞带，佩鞶囊、弓及弓套，下身着月白色细口裤，脚穿灰褐色高靿靴。其右手勒住缰绳，牵马缓行，侧身扭脸面对后方另一人，似正在交谈。所牵灰绿色骏马颈下挂黑缨，络头齐全，鞍鞯俱备，胸前有攀胸，马鞍下披灰色障泥。后方一人年纪稍长，也是广额丰颐，椭圆形脸，浓眉大眼，高鼻梁。他头戴黑色圆形长裙帽，身穿赭红色圆领内衣，外罩赭色窄袖右衽长袍，着细口裤、黑色高靿靴，身侧紧随一匹枣红色马。二人轮廓线条勾勒清晰，衣褶自然流畅。马匹虽遮住人物部分身体，但透过马颈下部，仍可看到局部，形成前后层次的对比。马匹刻画细致，鼻唇勾画准确，眼神凝重，络头简洁，鬃毛、睫毛繁简得当，细而不乱。

回归图之鞍马导引图二　墓道东壁中层

Horseback Parade II of the Return Scene

Middle Section, East Wall of the Entry Ramp

此幅画面略残。画中人物均为胡须较长的长者，丰额广颐，椭圆形脸，头戴黑色圆形长裙帽，身穿白色圆领内衣，外罩深色或浅色右衽长袍，着黑色靴，腰间束蹀躞带，佩长剑。其中右上角一人回首后顾，其他人均目视前方，神情专注。近排一匹灰色骏马，双耳高竖，颈部齐鬃，肥腰圆臀，体型健壮。此马鞍鞯俱备，马鞍下披挂赭色虎皮障泥，马鞍上盖三叶纹浅红底软缎。此类纹饰在伊朗和阿富汗等国家常见。

驼队图 墓道东壁上层

Camel Caravan Scene

Upper Section, East Wall of the Entry Ramp

此幅表现的是驼队运载货物的场景。画面涣漫不清，仅可见三匹骆驼体型高大，四肢壮硕有力，正稳步前行。前一骆驼背上有鞍架，里面满载货物，驮着三叶纹绣花软囊和卷卷丝绸。后一骆驼背上隐约可见虎形皮囊、长方形箱包和圆腹高圈足水壶。画师构思独特，将画面描绘得生动鲜活，形象准确，反映出其对丝路贸易的熟悉。

七人宾礼图　墓道西壁下层

Seven Officials Receiving Guests Scene

Lower Section, West Wall of the Entry Ramp

此幅画面上共七人，为一组礼宾官员群像。七个人地位不同、等级不同、身份不同。画师把每个人的姿态神情，甚至内心都刻画出来了。前排正中一人广额丰颐，椭圆脸，浓眉凤眼，高鼻梁，小嘴，八字胡，连鬓络腮胡。他头戴黑色山字形鲜卑帽，身穿赭黄色圆领窄袖右衽缺胯长袍，腰束黑色蹀躞带，佩弓、弓囊、剑、矢箙和鞶囊。据服装、配饰推测，地位似乎较其他人稍高。前排最右侧的中年人，神情恭敬且目光专注，似乎随同一起迎接宾客。后排最左侧的中年人双手扶旗杆，但侧脸看向鼓吹者的方向；后排左侧第二位中年人手扶旗杆，身子与头转向其右侧，目光似被远处事物所吸引；旁边三人相互凑近，似在小声交谈。

鼓吹图　墓道西壁下层

Military Band Performing Scene

Lower Section, West Wall of the Entry Ramp

此幅绘有四人对吹长角。左侧二人为正面，广额丰颐，椭圆形脸，浓眉凤眼，高鼻梁，小嘴。他们头戴黑色山字形风帽，身穿月白色圆领窄袖左衽长袍，着灰白色细口裤、黑色靴，腰间束红色蹀躞带，挂有黑色鞶囊和长剑。右侧二人为背面，衣裳颜色为赭红色，服饰、姿势基本相同。四人均用右手紧紧将长角的义嘴按在嘴唇边，左手向左前方伸直，用力高举长角号筒。四个吹角手昂首鼓腹，奋力劲吹，提起脚跟，脚尖点地，由于用力过猛，脸部腮帮子鼓起，脸色通红。

长角，又称大角，鲜卑人称之为簸逻回，多用作吹奏军阵之乐、征战之音，音色抑扬顿挫，澎湃激昂。鼓吹是汉魏时期对功勋卓著者的赏赐，有骑吹、立吹之分，可作迎宾之乐、行军之乐。

鼓吹图　墓道东壁下层

Military Band Performing Scene

Lower Section, East Wall of the Entry Ramp

此幅因所处位置与西壁正相对，可以相互参照。东壁所绘吹角手姿态与西壁基本相同，脸部腮帮鼓起，脸色通红，昂首鼓腹。但手的姿势和西壁正相反。他们用左手将长角的义嘴按在嘴唇边，右手向前伸出，托举着长角号筒。右侧吹者的后边有二马，可见鞍鞯边垂下的马镫。这为我们提供了北齐时期马镫的具体图像资料。

这组吹角人物形象生动，充分体现了画师的技法，让观者如身临其境，真切感受到吹奏长角的欢乐情景。观其局部细节，可以看出乐器重叠处的线条处理并不十分准确，出现了错位。

鼓吹图（局部） 墓道东壁下层

Details of Military Band Performing Scene

Lower Section, East Wall of the Entry Ramp

门官仪卫一 / 门官仪卫二 墓门外东、西侧壁

Ceremonial Guards I & II

East and West Sidewalls outside the Tomb Door

此为两幅门官仪卫图。

此二门官皆头戴梁冠，广额丰颐，椭圆脸，前庭饱满，浓眉大眼，高颧骨，高鼻梁，嘴唇微开，连鬓络腮胡，长须飘逸。身着朱红色大袖衫，拖于地，外披裲裆，下露笏头履。他们身形高大挺拔，神情庄重肃穆，虽褒衣博带，却掩盖不住游牧民族纵横草原的刚健和骁勇，同时还兼具华夏汉文化推崇的纯粹和雅致。

在左侧门官朝服肩部和胸部可见“朱”字残留。据此推断壁画概由专人按照粉本用淡墨起底稿线，“朱”字即是提醒后面上色者要以朱色敷彩。

细观右侧门官，尤为精彩！脸部敷彩，呈现出浓淡的立体层次；脖颈后寥寥几笔，勾画出肌肤肉感；胡须毛发，一丝不苟；衣裳褶皱，线条自然流畅。

门官仪卫一（局部） 墓门外东侧壁

Details of Ceremonial Guard I

East Sidewall outside the Tomb Door

门官仪卫二 （局部） 墓门外西侧壁

Details of Ceremonial Guard II

West Sidewall outside the Tomb Door